Design and Make
CARDS

Helen Greathead

W
FRANKLIN WATTS
LONDON • SYDNEY

Contents

A card for every occasion

Do you like giving and receiving cards? People have been sending cards for centuries, but in the last 150 years they have become big business around the world. In this book, we show you how to make cards with things you can find around your home. There are ideas for pop-up cards, fabric cards, and even cards inspired by nature.

Valentine's verse

The earliest European greetings cards were Valentine's Day (14th February) cards. Back in the Middle Ages lovers used to sing Valentine's verses to each other. But after 1400, they started to send messages in cards. These were made by hand and often very fancy! Some cards were folded and cut into lace patterns, others had stencilled pictures on them.

Kate Greenaway

Kate Greenaway was a children's author and illustrator, but she also designed greetings cards. Her first Valentine's card, published in 1868, sold 25,000 copies!

Christmas cards

In 1843, an Englishman called Henry Cole sent the very first Christmas card. He wanted to remind his friends to think about the poor during the festive season. So the first Christmas card was also the first charity card.

In the United States of America, the first Christmas card was produced in 1851, but the idea took another 20 years to catch on. New printing techniques, and the arrival of the American penny post system in 1873, started a card-sending trend that is still growing!

Celebrations

Today, people in countries all over the world send cards to celebrate birthdays and festivals. Many people send cards at New Year, and for their own religious festivals, such as the Hindu festival of Diwali or Jewish Hanukkah. Now we can even send e-cards for every occasion!

Using your imagination

In this book, we encourage you to look at shop-bought cards and cards from around the world for inspiration, and to think about ways of making your own. Use the techniques we suggest and your own imagination to see what you can do. Giving a card is so much more special when you can say you made it yourself!

Season's Greetings

Be prepared

Here is a collection of things you will need to make the cards in this book. You can collect things gradually and store them in a large box.

Tips

* Always read the instructions all the way through BEFORE you start.
* Clear plenty of space to work.
* Always try laying things out before you stick them down.
* Take time to think about your ideas. If you get stuck, flick through books or magazines for inspiration, or discuss your ideas with a friend.

Things to collect

A cutting knife and cutting board – always get an adult to help you when using a knife

Pencil sharpener

Eraser

PVA glue

Hole punch

Set square

Double-sided sticky tape, masking tape and sticky pads

Tracing paper

For cutting and sticking: a variety of cards and papers (different colours and thicknesses), foils (sticky backed if possible), coloured tissue paper, scraps of shiny or holographic wrapping paper, scraps of fabric with interesting textures.

Glitter glue

Glue stick

Wax crayons

Scissors

Felt-tip pens ballpoint pens (see opposite)

Metallic pens

Pencils

6

Other useful bits and pieces:

Dried leaves,
flowers, grasses

Stars and sequins

Stick-on eyes

Paper fasteners

Ribbon

Stencils

Useful techniques and ideas

✳ To cut straight lines, use a lined cutting board, or tape some squared paper onto a board. Line your work up with the squares on the board and use a set square, or ruler, to mark or cut lines.

✳ Score the folds of each card by using an empty ballpoint pen case (remove the ink tube and nib). Run the pen down the side of a ruler to keep the line straight. Then fold the card and press down.

You don't have to be brilliant at drawing to make these cards! Instead you can:
✳ Trace over pictures from books or magazines.
✳ Cut out pictures from magazines or wrapping paper.
✳ Draw stick pictures.
✳ Draw simple patterns.

Here's MY card

Some people carry business cards as an easy way to pass on their business details to new contacts. In some parts of the world, people give cards with their personal details to their friends.

Look at this!

This design is really simple, but it isn't as easy to make as it looks.

dci
decorated cakes inc
Icing House
Butter Lane
Devon DV20 7ML

Telephone: 019-275-02840

✳ What do you notice first when you look at the card?

✳ How else could you use a second colour?

Design and select

Design a personal card for yourself. Think carefully about how much information you will include. Sketch some simple pictures of yourself. Look at letters and numbers in old magazines and cut some out.

Challenge
What other image could you use on your card?

Make

1 Use masking tape to fix a sheet of tracing paper over the top of some squared paper. With a pencil and ruler, mark out the size of your card on the tracing paper. Make it no bigger than 90mm long and 55 mm high.

90mm

55mm

2 Use the squared lines to draw a border, if you are using one. Cut out the picture you drew earlier and select letters and numbers from the ones you cut out. Place your picture, and the words and numbers under the tracing paper; spell out your name and any other information you want on your card.

0033 377 7667

A few points to think about

- Try to leave plenty of space between the card edge, or border, and your picture or lettering.
- Make sure the letters are evenly spaced
- Make sure the lettering is not too close to the drawing.

3 Play around with the picture and words until you are happy with your layout. Then, go over the design in pen on the tracing paper. Don't draw the very edge of the card, just mark where the corners are. Once the ink is dry, you can rub out the pencil lines and admire your design.

Challenge
How else could you put lettering on your card?

4 Ask for permission to use a photocopier to make eight copies of your design. Carefully cut out your cards, using the corner marks as a guide and stick these onto a stronger piece of card. Now cut out your finished cards. Your friends will be impressed!

Challenge
Can you think of a way to use a second colour on your card?

9

Nature card

You don't have to draw at all to make a really stunning card. Just use natural things like leaves and grasses, but take time to get your design just right.

Design and select

Collect a selection of leaves and grasses. Place them on plain card first to work out how you will arrange them. Then select the paper you will use. We've chosen handmade paper with rough edges, to match the natural theme, and then mounted it onto stronger card.

Make

1 Prepare your materials. We used dried grasses and leaves and pressed them by putting them between sheets of blotting paper, with a pile of heavy books on top. It takes a couple of weeks to dry the leaves.

Challenge
How else can you preserve leaves or flowers?

2 Cut out a rectangle of card twice the size you want your card to be. Score down the middle using a ruler and an empty ballpoint pen.

3 Cut out your handmade paper so that it fits over the front of the card and glue it on.

4 Decide where the leaves will go and how you will attach them to the card. We cut small holes in the leaves and the front of the card. Then we loosely knotted the grasses, threaded them through the holes and fixed them with tape on the inside of the card.

Challenge
What could you use to make the leaves shiny?

11

Fold and fold again!

You can make a card really stand out by simply folding it in three. Use it for a party invite and you can even make a detachable reply slip!

Design and select

Design a card which folds into three sections. Use a simple shape to create an effective pop-out image. Think about how you will use colour and sketch out some ideas.

Make

1 Divide a long piece of card into four sections by drawing three lines from top to bottom. Make sure the sections are all the same size. Draw your design so it crosses the first line you have drawn.

cut line

1   2   3

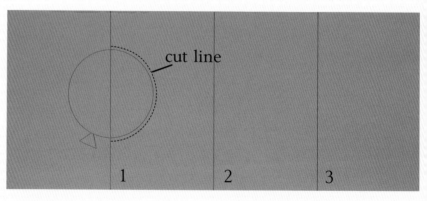

2 Score all the way down the middle line (2) using an empty ballpoint pen. Now score down the first line (1) above and below your design, but not through it. Then ask for help to cut carefully around the right-hand side of your shape, as shown (left).

3 Next, decorate your picture. We cut a circle and a small triangle out of holographic foil to make the balloon shape, and stuck them on.

4 Fold the card down the first and middle lines and try your pop-up. Mark the third line to show that it is detachable and to make your reply slip. We used a gold pen to draw a dotted line.

Challenge
We used the fourth section to make a reply slip. How else could you use this section of your card?

5 Write your message on the card – perhaps use a stencil for the important words. In case you make a mistake, it's a good idea to stencil onto some white card first, then cut out the words and stick them onto the invitation.

6 If you decide to mark lines to write inside the invitation, be careful to draw them lightly in pencil first so you can rub them out if you make a mistake. Finally, try out the full effect!

Cuddly cloth card

A fabric card always looks special. Here's how they make them in Bolivia, South America.

Bolivia is famous for its colourful textiles. This card was handmade using a frame to create the shape of a dove on the fabric.

✱ How do the colours chosen help the image to stand out?

Design and select

Make a card using soft fabric and a shaped frame. First choose your fabric. Try out a few sketches and choose your shape. Simple is best! We've made a card for a new baby.

Make

1 Cut out a rectangle of card to the size you want your card to be. Draw your shape onto the card, leaving at least 2cm between the drawing and the edge of the card.

2cm

2 With an adult's help, use scissors to cut your shape out of the card; discard the middle. Now use a gold pen to draw round your shape to outline it.

14

3 Cut a rectangular piece of fabric larger than the shape and just smaller than your card. Put a thin layer of PVA glue on the card, and press it gently onto the fabric.

4 Now add the features to the bear. Use different coloured material to make the nose and ears and stick them on the teddy, using a thin layer of PVA glue. Add some plastic eyes.

Challenge
How could you adapt this card so it is padded?

5 You need to attach the frame to a folded piece of card so that it can stand up. Cut out a piece of card that, when folded in half, is a little larger than your fabric frame. Attach the fabric and frame to the card using double-sided tape. Using a gold pen, draw a thin border round the card to finish it off.

Challenge
Use this technique to make a really colourful Hanukkah card.

Photo frame card

Do your parents send photos of you to your relatives? Why not turn them into greetings cards?

Design and select

Design a photo card to send to a relative; include a short message on the front. Look at some photographs of yourself; which one will work best as a card? How will you add your message?

Make

1 Put tracing paper over the photograph, and lightly mark the area you are going to use. Work out how big your frame needs to be and mark the corners of your photograph, as shown above. We also added a speech bubble shape.

Challenge
Make a funny card by playing around with the words and photo. Can you make it on the computer?

2 Cut a piece of card for the frame. It needs to be three times the size of the outside of your frame. Fold the card into three equal parts.

3 Turn your tracing paper over and use masking tape to fix it in position on the middle section of card. Draw over your tracing to copy the frame, bubble shape and corners of the photograph onto the card. Make sure you get it the right way round. Remove the tracing paper.

4 Ask for help to cut around the frame and speech bubble using a craft knife; push out the middle. Line up your photo with the picture corner markers and tape it in position. Seal the bottom and middle sections together with double-sided tape. Fold over the last section so that the card stands up.

5 Write your message on a separate bit of paper shaped like a speech bubble. Cut it out and stick it down. Draw a border using a gold pen around the photo. Write a further message inside your card. Now your card is ready to post!

Hello

Hel

Challenge How else could you decorate the frame?

A message with a bounce!

It's fun to send cards that move. We've used a really simple technique to make this witch bounce up and down on her broomstick!

Design and select

Design a card with a part that bounces! Sketch out your idea and decide which part will move up and down. How will you make the bouncing mechanism? We made a Hallowe'en card with a bouncing witch. Select your materials — we used card for the witch and sequins for decoration.

Make

1 Trace your witch from your drawing onto a piece of dark card. Cut out the main shape of your witch. Using different coloured card, cut out separate pieces for the features, including the broomstick. Carefully glue them onto your witch.

2 Select your card for the background. Cut out a large piece of the card, making sure the witch fits over the top.

Challenge
Can you give a shape to the background, too?

3 Next, take a piece of strong plastic — we used part of a thin plastic file (for holding paper) — and cut it into a short strip. Bend the strip in half and press down, so that the two parts stay slightly open.

Challenge
The folded plastic makes the witch bounce. Can you think of another way to do this?

4 Using sticky pads, connect one side of the plastic strip to the witch and the other side to the card.

5 Decorate the background of your card with cut-out shapes, like stars and moons. We used sequins for the stars and card for the moon.

Challenge
Use this technique to make a get well card.

Pop-up card

A pop-up card makes your pictures come to life: simple designs work best.

Design and select

Design a pop-up card for a special occasion. Draw a picture of your idea. How will you add colour to your picture? We made a card for someone who is moving house.

Look at this!

You'll be surprised where you can find ideas! This children's book has a pop-up picture on every page.

✱ How do you think the mechanism works?

Make

1 Work out the size of your card and cut two pieces of flexible card exactly the same size. Score a line down the middle of both cards using an empty ballpoint pen barrel (see page 7). Put one piece aside.

2 With an adult's help, carefully cut two horizontal slits across the fold of the card using a craft knife. Make sure the slits are the same length and same distance from the edge of the card.

3 Score two lines down the card from either end of the slits to make a rectangle shape in the middle. Fold the card in half, pushing the rectangle inside the card.

4 Measure the card and draw your picture to fit it. Cut out the picture. Put in any background details on the card then stick your picture to the pop-up rectangle.

5 Stick the second piece of card that you set aside earlier onto the back of your pop-up to finish it off. Now you can add your message!

Challenge

Design a peephole through the front of the card that gives a hint of what's inside.

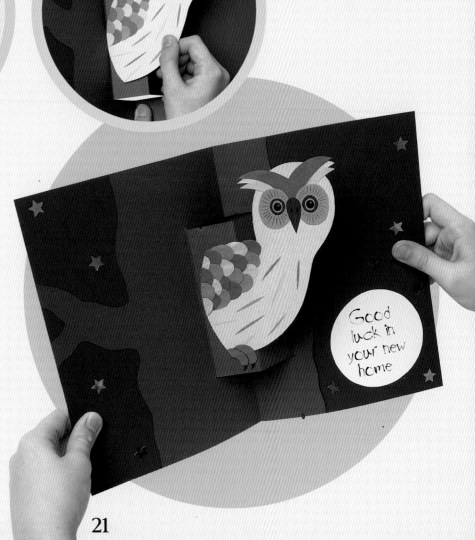

Good luck in your new home

Easy batik

Sometimes you need to make lots of cards the same, like at Christmas, or for party invites or thank you cards. Here's a quick and easy way of doing it.

Look at this Indian Christmas card which uses a technique called batik. Batik is made by painting wax pictures on fabric. When the fabric is dyed, the waxed parts don't take the colour.

✳ How do you think the wax is applied?

Design and select

Design a simple, shaped card — we've made a bauble you can hang on a Christmas tree — and choose some coloured card. Sketch out a pattern to decorate your card. To create a batik effect, we've used wax crayons and thinned paint.

Make

1 Cut the main shape out of card and use a hole punch to make a hole in the top so it will hang up. Use your first shape as a template so you can cut out as many cards as you need.

2 Take a couple of sheets of good-quality paper. We chose white writing paper. Select a range of wax crayons and try them out on the paper. Try different colours and shapes to make patterns.

3 Use paint which has been thinned with water and lightly cover the patterns with it — really experiment. Then, when you are pleased with the effect, paint a whole sheet.

Challenge
How could you adapt this technique to make a picture card instead?

4 Cut interesting shapes from the patterned paper and glue them to your cut-out cards. We added a few dabs from a glitter pen to make the bauble sparkle.

5 Thread some gold ribbon through the hole in the card. Write a greeting on the other side. Now your friends can hang it on their tree!

Challenge
How would you make envelopes to fit these cards?

Spinning card

You can make a card with a moving picture using a rotating disk inside the card. We've created a flickering diya lamp to send at Diwali, the Indian festival of lights.

Look at this!

Candles are used for all sorts of celebrations, from religious festivals to birthdays.

✳ How can you make a card that flickers like a candle?

✳ Apart from Diwali cards, what other cards could you make featuring candles?

Design and select

Make a card with a moving picture. Sketch out your design and choose your materials. We used black card, shiny card, tissue paper and a gold pen. Use a paper fastener to make it spin.

Make

1 Cut out a large square of card, about 30x30cm. Using an empty ballpoint pen (see page 7), score lines down the card to divide it into quarters and then fold it up. Cut a small semi-circle out of the front edge.

2 To make the spinning disc, cut out a circle in thicker card that is slightly smaller than your folded card. Ask for help to make a hole in the centre of the spinner. Unfold the card and make another hole in the centre of the bottom right section. Push a paper fastener through the hole in the spinner and the hole in the card and fix in position.

3 With the card unfolded, work out where your flame will go on the front and cut out a flame shape. Ask for help to do this.

4 To create the flame effect, cut out circles in shiny gold and red card and stick them onto the spinner.

5 Cut out shapes to make the diya (the pot that holds a Diwali light). We cut the shapes from tissue paper and stuck them on with glue. Decorate the card with gold pen. Now spin the card to make the flames flicker!

Challenge
How could you adapt this technique to make different pictures appear on the card?

A card that grows

It's always lovely to give flowers.
Here are some that actually grow!

Design and select

Make a collage card with flowers that really grow!
Cut out shapes and images that you like from old
magazines and newspapers and arrange them in a
'patchwork' picture. Think about where you will
position your flowers and pots.

Make

1 Cut out a rectangle
of coloured card and
stick on the background
details. We used different
shades of red to make
bricks and a window cut
from a magazine. Next
stick your flower pots onto
your window sill.

Challenge
What else could you use
to make the collage?

2 Get an adult to help you to make a small slit at the top of each flower pot with a craft knife. Cut out T-shaped strips to fix the flowers onto.

Challenge

Could you make the flower grow tall enough to write your message on the stalk?

3 Now slot the strips of card through the slits. Experiment with the position of the flowers on the strips at the front of the card. Do you want all the flowers to grow to the same height?

Challenge

What else could you put on your card that grows?

4 Stick the flower heads onto the strips of card, and cut the strips to fit, leaving tabs at the top to pull the flowers up. Mount your design onto a large sheet of folded card. Now you have a growing flower card!

27

A kissing card

People have been sending Valentine's cards for hundreds of years! This one has a special sliding mechanism. Pull the tab to make the couple kiss!

Design and select

Design a Valentine's card with a sliding mechanism. Think carefully about the materials you will need and sketch out a few ideas. We've used different colours and thicknesses of card.

Make

1 You will need to cut out one piece of card for the background of your picture, and a larger piece to make the folding part of the card. Decide what your background will be. We used a red heart on black card.

2 Use a long piece of card to make the sliding mechanism. Fold the card in half lengthways, draw an L-shape, cut it out and glue the two sides together.

3 Draw, colour and cut out your two faces. Stick the boy onto the background card. Place the girl's face in position, but don't stick it down.

4 Cut a slit for the sliding mechanism in the background picture. To work out the length of the slit (C) you need to measure the width of the tab (A) and add this to the distance between the lips (B). Remove the left face before cutting your slit with a craft knife. Get an adult to help with this.

5 Place the long section of your L-shape behind your background and push the short part up through the slit. Stick a strip of card along the bottom of the mechanism to hold it in place.

Challenge
How else could you make sure the mechanism is held in place?

6 On the front of the card, stick the girl's face onto the short part of the L-shape. Pull the tab to make sure the faces meet, but don't overlap. Use double-sided tape to attach the background to the main folding card; make sure you don't stick the tab down as well. Now you can add your decorations.

Challenge
Can you reverse the slide effect, to make an Easter card with an egg that hatches?

29

Glossary

adapt
make suitable for your purpose

collage
picture made by putting together scraps of paper and other things

detach
to remove something that was fixed to something else

diya
clay lamps containing a candle or oil used in Diwali, the Hindu festival of lights

e-card
an electronic card that can be sent in an email

feature
detail; an important part of something

Hanukkah
a Jewish festival held in December

holographic
something that appears to be three-dimensional

inspiration
something that gives you ideas

layout
the arrangement or design of something

mount
to put a picture onto a piece of card, or into an album

stencil, stencilled
a piece of card with pieces cut out of it; used to make a picture or design

textiles
different types of cloth, such as wool, nylon or denim

Further information

You might find these websites helpful for finding ideas, techniques and materials:

www.emotionscards.com/ museum/museum.html
– a virtual museum of historical greetings cards. Looking at some ingenious cards from the past can help to give you great ideas for the present.

www.thegardener.btinternet.co.uk/ preserving.html
Includes a number of ways you can preserve flowers and leaves – ask an adult to help you!

www.webindia123.com/craft/ paint/batik/batik.html
Information about how Indian batik is made, and a few samples to look at.

http://cgee.hamline.edu/see/ goldsworthy/see_an_andy.html
Visit this artist's website to find more ideas for using natural materials.

www.crayola.com
Visit this site for craft ideas, to view new craft materials and to find out where to buy them, and to create your own e-cards.

www.childrensscrapstore.co.uk
Information about the children's scrapstore in Bristol, where scrap materials are recycled and sold for educational art and craft projects. Also includes a list of other scrapstores around the UK.

www.enform.supanet.com/ scrapstores.htm
A directory of UK scrapstores.

www.devon.gov.uk/index/learning/ early_years_and_childcare/ disc_services/toylibr.htm
More scrapstore addresses!

Every effort has been made by the Publisher to ensure that these websites are suitable for children, and contain no inappropriate or offensive material. However, because of the nature of the Internet, it is impossible to guarantee that the contents of these sites will not be altered. We strongly advise that Internet access is supervised by a responsible adult.

Index

First published in 2005 by
Franklin Watts, 96 Leonard Street
London, EC2A 4XD

Franklin Watts Australia
45-51 Huntley Street, Alexandria, NSW 2015

Copyright © 2005 Franklin Watts

Editor: Rachel Tonkin Art Director: Jonathan Hair
Design: Matthew Lilly and Anna-Marie D'Cruz Photography: Steve Sho

Picture credits: Mary Evans PL/Alamy: 4tr. Popperfoto/Alamy: 5t. V & A
Images/Alamy: 4bl. Every attempt has been made to clear copyright. Shou
there be any inadvertent omission please apply to the publisher for rectificat
With thanks to Patricia Greathead for the loan of the cards on pages 5, 14 and

A CIP catalogue record for this book
is available from the British Library

Dewey classification: 745.594'1

ISBN 0 7496 6074 0

Printed in Hong Kong/China